DIGITAL CITIZENS

COMMUNITY
AND
MEDIA

By Ben Hubbard

Illustrated by Diego Vaisberg

W
FRANKLIN WATTS
LONDON • SYDNEY

Franklin Watts
First published in Great Britain in 2018 by
The Watts Publishing Group
Copyright © The Watts Publishing
Group 2018

Credits
Series Editor: Julia Bird
Illustrator: Diego Vaisberg
Packaged by: Collaborate

ISBN 978 1 4451 6159 4

Every attempt has been made to clear copyright.
Should there be any inadvertent omission please
apply to the publisher for rectification.

Franklin Watts
An imprint of
Hachette Children's Group
Part of The Watts Publishing Group
Carmelite House
50 Victoria Embankment
London EC4Y 0DZ

An Hachette UK Company
www.hachette.co.uk
www.franklinwatts.co.uk

Printed in China

FSC
www.fsc.org

MIX
Paper from
responsible sources
FSC® C104740

CONTENTS

WHAT IS DIGITAL CITIZENSHIP?

When we log onto the internet we become part of a giant, online world.

In this world we can use our phones, tablets and computers to explore, create and communicate with billions of different people. Together, these people make up a global digital community. That is why they are known as digital citizens. When you use the internet you are a digital citizen too. So what does this mean?

CITIZEN VS DIGITAL CITIZEN

A good citizen is someone who behaves well, looks after themselves and others, and tries to make their community a better place. A good digital citizen acts exactly the same way. However, the online world is bigger than just a local neighbourhood, city or country. It spans the whole world and crosses every kind of border. It is therefore up to all digital citizens everywhere to make this digital community a safe, fun and exciting place for everyone.

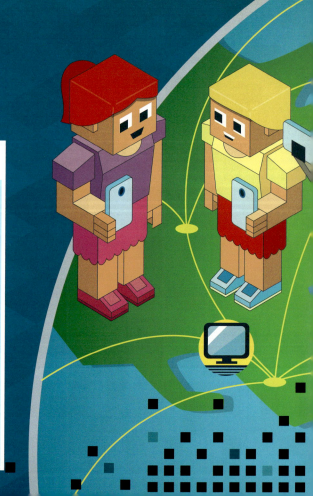

MY DIGITAL COMMUNITY AND MEDIA

The global digital community is like a huge web made up of smaller networks and groups. Its members connect with each other using social media, forums, hobbyist websites and gaming sites. However, clever digital citizens are smart about socialising online. This is how they enjoy their digital community and media safely.

SOCIAL SOCIETY

How do you connect with other people online?
Do you use social media, or are you a gamer? Are you a hobbyist
with special interests, or a text-talker who loves forums and
chat rooms? Perhaps you are not even sure what some of these
things are. Don't worry: they are all explained below.

SOCIAL MEDIA

Websites and apps that allow people to share posts, photos
and videos are known as social media. Social media sites are
usually free, but they require users to register and log-
in to use them. Many people stay in touch with friends and
family on social media sites and meet new people there too.

GAMING

Playing games over the internet, often against multiple
players, is known as gaming. Gamers play against others from
all over the world and can interact with them by sending
messages or chatting live over headsets. Often, a large
network of people is formed around a single popular game.

FORUMS

Internet forums are discussion websites where people have text conversations with others online. A forum often features different topic categories, commonly known as threads. Forums are not always live, unlike chat rooms. In a chat room, people log-in to have text conversations together in real time.

HOBBYISTS

Hobbyist websites are for people who share a passion for a particular hobby or interest, from crafting to birdwatching to miniature model-making. Often a hobbyist website includes its own forum or chat room, and links to helpful websites.

MY NETWORKS

Did you know hundreds of millions of young people have a social media account?

Many social media sites are just for children, but young people can also often join adult social media sites too. Some of these sites say their members must be at least 13 years of age, but others have no restrictions. So how do you know if you're old enough to join and how should you stay safe in the social media world?

WHAT ARE YOU DOING?

OPENING A SOCIAL MEDIA ACCOUNT.

CAN I OPEN ONE TOO?

SORRY, YOU'RE TOO YOUNG FOR THIS SITE.

TRUSTED TALK

Talking to a trusted adult about joining an adult social media site is the best first step. If they think you're too young for a particular site, they can help you find one that is more suitable. Make your trusted adult one of your 'friends', so they can help you along the way.

PRIVACY SETTINGS

Once you've agreed on a social media site, your trusted adult can help you with its privacy settings. These control who can see your posts, blogs, videos and photos. Choosing a 'friends only' privacy setting is best. Make sure to check the privacy settings regularly, as websites sometimes change their policies.

PAUSE BEFORE POSTING

Even with a privacy setting of 'friends only', others may be able to see what you post on social media. It's therefore important not to post anything that may upset or embarrass you, or anyone you know. Such posts might include a silly photo, or a comment that could hurt someone's feelings. A quick pause to think before you post can help prevent you uploading something you'll later regret.

I WONDER HOW I CHANGE THE PRIVACY SETTINGS ON THIS?

BY CLICKING HERE AND HERE. AND YOU CAN UPLOAD YOUR AVATAR HERE. SEE?

RESPECT OTHERS

Good digital citizens always respect others on social media. This means being polite, friendly and kind. If someone is not behaving this way towards you, you can block them from your social media account.

STAY SECRET

It's important not to post anything that gives away your personal information, or that of your friends. Personal information includes your name, phone number and address. You can also use a screen name and avatar for your account to protect your identity.

GAMING GROUPS

Gaming websites are exciting places where you can enjoy the action with players from around the world.

However, they are more than just play areas. They are also places you can interact with others who love the same games as you. This is why online gaming makes up one of the largest networks of the internet. Staying safe and protected while you are gaming is therefore key.

THIS IS AWESOME. IT'S LIKE ANOTHER WORLD!

LOADS OF THE SAME PEOPLE SHOW UP HERE EVERY WEEK.

WHICH GAME?

Online games aren't all first-person shooters or quest games. There are also sports, strategy, fitness and family games that require a range of different playing skills. Have a look around online to find some games you can play with your trusted adult or others at home.

BLOCK THE BULLY

Bullying can happen in gaming, just as it does in the real world, in the form of nasty messages or even threats from other players. 'Griefing' is a form of bullying where other players harass you or destroy things you have built in an online game. The simplest way to deal with these bullies is to block them, or change the game's settings so only people you know can join in with you.

PERSONAL PRIVACY AND PREDATORS

Gaming sites require users to have a screen name and avatar to protect their personal identity. It's also important never to give away details about yourself or your location. Sometimes predators can target children through online gaming. If someone is being extra nice to you, asking you lots of questions and offering things for free, it is best not to trust them. Block them if they persist.

HOBBIES AND INTERESTS

Have you ever felt like you were the only person in the world that liked a particular thing, such as a certain toy, book or film?

In the online world there is almost certainly someone who likes it just as much as you! This is why the internet is a great place to unite people with specific hobbies, subjects and interests. It can help new people become interested too.

WHICH WEBSITE?

There are a vast number of websites online dedicated to a specific subject, hobby or interest. These can be about almost anything — from slot-car racing to arcade games from the 1980s. Websites can also be run by a group dedicated to a particular thing, called a club or association. It's usually easy to become a member, but always check with your trusted adult first.

STAY IN TOUCH?

Websites dedicated to a particular interest or hobby often keep in touch with their members through email newsletters. Sometimes these are nice things to receive. At other times there may be too many emails, or your email address may be passed on to other people. For this reason, it is important not to give out your email address unless you are sure how it will be used.

BEWARE THE BILL

It's easy to spend money on 'extras' on websites dedicated to a special hobby. Before you agree to purchasing anything, make sure you have your trusted adult's consent. The simplest thing is to never fill out any bank details on a website or agree to anything that might cost money.

THEY SAY THIS TROMBONE OIL IS GREAT STUFF. CAN I BUY SOME?

BUT YOU DON'T OWN A TROMBONE.

WEIRD AND WONDERFUL HOBBYIST WEBSITES

ToyVoyagers — a website that sends your stuffed toy on trips around the world and posts photos of their adventures.

Extreme Ironing International — a group that carries out ironing in strange and difficult situations, like mountain climbing or kayaking through rapids. The results are then posted online.

Weird Eggs — a website dedicated to strange-looking eggs, which members post photos of.

NETIQUETTE

Being a good digital citizen means treating people online as you do in the real world.

However, sometimes it's difficult in the online world to express what you mean. It's easy for misunderstandings to happen by accident. This is why you have to work harder in the online world to show you mean well and are being courteous and polite.

💬

WE'RE GOING TO KILL YOU AT THE GAME TODAY.

HUH?!

WHAT IS NETIQUETTE?

Netiquette is made up of the two words 'etiquette' and 'net', for the internet. Etiquette means the rules for behaving well. Here are some netiquette rules to follow:

1 Don't SHOUT by typing in capital letters.

2 Don't trade insults with people, which is known as 'flaming'.

AVOID MISUNDERSTANDINGS

When we talk to people in the real world, it's easy to make them understand us. Sometimes the way we say something or how we use our body language can show others whether we are joking or being serious. But online, we do not have access to these visual clues. Therefore, it's best to explain if you are being sarcastic or making a joke. You can easily do this by adding some emojis at the end of your sentence, or text clues such as ;-).

I MEAN: WE'RE GOING TO KILL YOU AT THE GAME TODAY!
😜😜😜

3 Check before you click, to make sure what you are saying is clear.

4 Respect the privacy of others.

5 Share your knowledge and help newbies if they don't know the rules.

KINDNESS, NOT CRUELTY

The online world is what digital citizens everywhere make it.

What we say and how we act creates the culture of this vast, digital community. In this way, it is like the real world. However, sometimes we feel hidden in the online world. This means we can be more likely to say things about people we might not say to their face.

SUZY ONLY SCORED THREE RUNS TODAY. SHE CAN'T BAT TO SAVE HER LIFE!

HMM, PERHAPS THAT SOUNDS A BIT HARSH. SHOULD I POST IT?

TOO QUICK TO CRITICISE

It's easy to quickly post a message, blog or comment criticising something or somebody — but would you like the same thing done to you? Being a good digital citizen means stopping to think before saying anything that might be thoughtless or unkind. Sometimes when you write something it may not seem like a big deal, but when it is published online it can make a huge impact.

WHAT ARE TROLLS?

Trolls are people who say nasty things about others online. Often they hide in wait in chat rooms and online forums before launching an attack. Some trolls don't think they are doing anything wrong. Others feel bold because they think the internet makes them anonymous. However, trolls do leave a trail behind and can be easily tracked down.

ONLINE NEWS

One of the benefits of being a digital citizen is accessing the news 24 hours a day.

This is because as soon as a news event breaks, it is online within minutes. Sometimes the news is broken on social media websites instead of by traditional news outlets. However, clever digital citizens know not to trust everything they read online and choose where their news comes from carefully.

WHERE'S MY NEWSPAPER? I NEED TO KNOW WHAT'S GOING ON IN THE WORLD!

TRADITIONAL NEWS

Traditional news outlets, such as newspapers, television and radio, can also be found online. These outlets hire professionally-trained journalists to gather and report the news. They are free to report the news without interference from politicians or business leaders.

ONLINE NEWS MEDIA

In the internet age, the news can be reported by anyone with an internet connection. Social media sites post news reports for their members. Microblogging services often post breaking news faster than the traditional news outlets. However, social media websites are not professional news organisations run by trained journalists. The news they report is therefore not always reliable.

INFORMATION OVERLOAD

The great number of news stories online can be overwhelming. The many terrible disasters, wars and life-threatening events can make it seem like the world is falling apart. However, global events like this have been going on since the dawn of human history. The only difference is that now we can find out about them almost instantly online.

SPOT THE FAKE

In the modern world, digital citizens are often fed false news stories known as 'fake news'.

Fake news is written by people in order to mislead others. Some people publish fake news during elections to make their opponents look bad. Others do it for financial gain. Fake news can be dangerous when lots of people believe it to be true. However, it's easy to spot fake news by following the tips below.

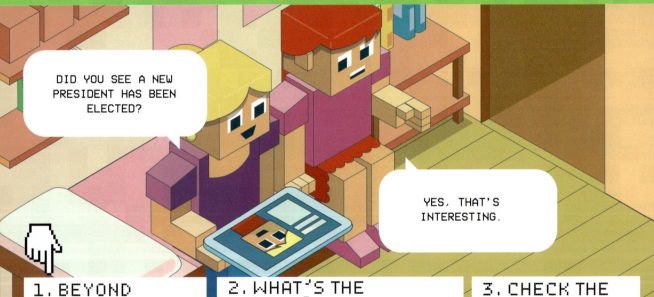

DID YOU SEE A NEW PRESIDENT HAS BEEN ELECTED?

YES, THAT'S INTERESTING.

1. BEYOND THE HEADLINE

Fake news headlines often grab your attention by making bold statements and inserting exclamation marks. But by reading on, it often becomes quickly apparent the stories are not real.

2. WHAT'S THE SOURCE?

What website was the story published on originally? Is it a real website from a news organisation? Or is the web address simply made to look like it belongs to a real news organisation? Check the 'About' section to check if a website is a fake. If there are no contact details except a 'gmail' account, then it's probably fake.

3. CHECK THE AUTHOR

By typing the author's name into a search engine you can quickly uncover whether they are a real journalist, or even a real person.

4. SPELLING MISTAKES

Spelling mistakes and messy layouts are a dead giveaway that a news article or the website it is posted on has been created by an amateur.

5. CHECK SOURCES

Are real news organisations also reporting the news you are reading? Are people quoted in the story? Are these quotes real, and are they real people? It's easy to find out by doing an online search on the quotes, the names and the news itself. If the search engine results only lead you back to the same article, it's a good sign that it's a fake.

6. NEWS OR ADVERT?

Sometimes advertisements are dressed up to look like news stories and used on a real news site. These are not 'fake news', but it's easy to mistake them for real news. Often they have an 'advertisement' or 'sponsored content' label to warn you they are not news, but not always.

I AM A BRAND

Popular social media sites are easy to recognise.

This is because they market themselves as a brand. This means their logo, name and colours are easily identifiable as belonging to that company. But did you know that when you use social media you are like a brand too? So what does your brand say about you?

LOOK YOURSELF UP

Have you ever typed your name into a search engine to see what pops up? You might find out about some other people who share the same name. But there may also be links to some of your photos, blogs and the other things you've posted online. All of these things make up your 'digital identity', which is all the information about you on the internet.

DIGITALLY DOWN

Your digital identity is made up of anything uploaded to the internet which is linked to your name. You can think about these things as being a part of your own personal brand. It's important to make this brand positive and show only the best things about yourself. This is because once something appears online, it's almost impossible to remove it. This means only posting things you'll always be happy for the world to see. An embarrassing photo may not seem like much now but it could have an impact later on in life.

UNITING ONLINE

The online world is a great way of uniting people from small communities and minorities in the real world.

They may be people from different ethnic or religious backgrounds, or those with special needs or alternative lifestyles. By finding others like themselves online, those who feel alone or on the outside of society can be more included.

SPECIAL NEEDS

The internet can be an empowering tool for those with special needs. Texting and messaging apps are a helpful technology for deaf people, for example. Before the internet, deaf people had to rely on fax machines instead of telephones for fast, long distance communication. This is one way internet technologies can help everyone participate more easily in our society.

MINORITY MILLIONS

The real world is made up of millions of different minorities. Minorities are those from groups that are different from mainstream society. These groups can have various religious, ethnic or cultural backgrounds. They may have a different sexual orientation or gender identity, such as those from the lesbian, gay, bisexual or transgender (LGBT) communities. People from minority groups can feel isolated and be discriminated against. However, social media can help them connect with each other and become more visible to the world. This helps fight against intolerance.

LOOK ISLA, THERE IS A LOCAL GROUP FOR DEAF PEOPLE LIKE US HERE.

SEEKING SUPPORT

It's easy to find a support group online if you need one. Maybe you've broken a leg and want to reach out to others who are also laid up. Maybe you've been suffering from a bad illness, or are just feeling down. Finding other people who are in the same position as you can make you feel much better. Otherwise it can be easy to feel alone.

SHRINKING THE WORLD

Social media is how digital citizens meet and learn about different people from all over the globe

Digital citizens know it is important to get along with everybody — regardless of nationality, colour or religion. This is how the online world is helping make the real world a more united, tolerant and joined-up place.

GEOGRAPHICAL ACCESS

Social media allows people from the most remote places to communicate with others elsewhere. Although not everywhere in the world has access to an internet connection yet, satellite technology is bringing the online world to more places than ever before. Digital citizens believe internet access for all people is important. It will also mean we can learn about the lives of people in the most distant places on the planet.

HI RUFINA!

TEACHING TOLERANCE

Digital citizens of the world understand everyone has to work together to make both the online and offline global community a better place. Often people who distrust or dislike others from different countries or cultures simply don't understand them. However, technologies such as social media are knocking down those barriers and showing everyone that people are really just the same, wherever they are from. Teaching tolerance is how digital citizens everywhere will change the world!

DIGITAL QUIZ

Now you've reached the end of this book, how do you feel about your digital community and media?

How much have you learned? And how much can you remember? Take this quiz and add up your score at the end to find out.

1. How old do some adult social media sites say members must be to join?
a. 13
b. 14
c. 12

2. Which of these is a common place people have text conversations with others online?
a. Forum
b. Chat house
c. Town square

3. Where on your social media account do you choose who can see your posts?
a. Public settings
b. Piracy settings
c. Privacy settings

4. What are the rules for being polite and showing manners online?
a. Netiquette
b. Croquette
c. Silhouette

5. People who trade insults with each other on social media are said to be …
a. Training
b. Flaming
c. Maiming

6. What is your digital identity?
a. A special picture ID with your name and address
b. Your avatar and screen name for gaming sites
c. All the things about you which can be seen online

7. What is it difficult to do once you've posted something online?
a. Delete it permanently
b. Look at it using your trusted adult's smartphone
c. Spread it everywhere on the internet

8. What do digital citizens think is important?
a. Digital access for everyone
b. Tolerance for all people online
c. Both of the above

HOW DID YOU DO? ADD UP YOUR SCORE TO SEE.

1-4: You are on your way but retake the quiz to get a score over 4.

5-7: You've passed the quiz well. Now see if you can pass the quiz in the book *My Digital Rights and Rules*.

8: Wow! 8 out of 8. You are a natural born digital citizen!

ANSWERS

1: a; 2: a; 3: c; 4: a; 5: a; 6: c;
7: a; 8: c

GLOSSARY

Apps
Short for 'applications', apps are computer programmes for mobile digital devices, such as smartphones or tablets.

Avatar
A computer icon or image that people use to represent themselves online.

Block
A way of stopping someone from sending you nasty messages, emails or texts online.

Cyberbullying
Bullying that takes place online or using internet-based apps.

Digital
Technology that involves computers.

Internet
The vast electronic network that allows billions of computers from around the world to connect to each other.

Online
Being connected to the internet via a computer or digital device.

Predator
A dangerous person who searches for other people to harm.

Privacy settings
Controls on social media websites that allow you to decide who has access to your profile and posts.

Screen name
Also known as a username, a screen name is a made-up name used to disguise your real identity, which is used for your online accounts.

Search engine
A computer programme that carries out a search of available information on the internet, based on the words you type in.

Smartphone
A mobile phone that is capable of connecting to the internet.

Social media
Websites that allow users to share content and information online.

Trusted adult
An adult you know well and trust who can help you with all issues relating to the internet.

Website
A collection of web pages that is stored on a computer and made available to people over the internet.

HELPFUL WEBSITES

Digital Citizenship
The following websites have helpful information about digital citizenship for young people:

www.digizen.org/kids/

www.digitalcitizenship.nsw.edu.au/
Prim_Splash/

www.cyberwise.org/digital-
citizenship-games

www.digitalcitizenship.net/Nine_
Elements.html

Bullying
These websites have excellent advice for kids who are experiencing bullying online. There are also some helplines, which children can call anonymously to receive expert help:

www.childline.org.uk/info-advice/
bullying-abuse-safety/types-
bullying/online-bullying/
Childline helpline for kids:
0800 1111

www.bullying.co.uk
BullyingUK helpline for kids:
0808 800 2222

www.stopbullying.gov/kids/facts/

www.commonsensemedia.org/videos/
cyberbullying-prevention-guide-for-
kids

Staying Safe
These websites are dedicated to keeping kids safe online, with lots of good advice:

www.childnet.com/young-people/
primary

www.kidsmart.org.uk

www.safetynetkids.org.uk/personal-
safety/staying-safe-online/

www.bbc.co.uk/newsround/13910067

INDEX

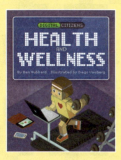

Health & Wellness

- What is digital citizenship?
- Your digital health and wellness
- Prepare to prevent pain
- Stretch, don't strain
- Digital training
- App attack
- Online time limits
- Online addiction
- Social media and self image
- Avoiding adverts
- Being boys and girls
- Digital detox
- Digital quiz

Rights & Rules

- What is digital citizenship?
- Know your rights
- Rule of the tools
- Information invasion
- Free speech
- Protecting others, protecting yourself
- Privacy particulars
- Digital law
- Original online work
- Illegal downloads
- Access for all
- Help everyone participate
- Digital quiz

My Digital World

- What is digital citizenship?
- Connect, collect and communicate
- A world of websites
- Cyber searching
- Digital friendships
- To share or not to share?
- Messaging aware
- Phone etiquette
- Cyberbullying
- Bystanding
- Send a cyber smile
- A world outside
- Digital quiz

My Digital Future

- What is digital citizenship?
- Future technology today
- Dating digital devices
- The latest thing
- Digital maintenance
- Explaining the world
- Online shopping
- Technology in business
- Technology in schools
- Educating the world
- Technology tomorrow
- The future is unwritten
- Digital quiz

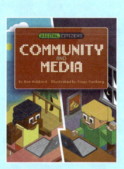

My Digital Community and Media

- What is digital citizenship?
- Social society
- My networks
- Gaming groups
- Hobbies and interests
- Netiquette
- Kindness, not cruelty
- Online news
- Spot the fake
- I am a brand
- Uniting online
- Shrinking the world
- Digital quiz

My Digital Safety and Security

- What is digital citizenship?
- Prepare to protect
- Trusted help
- Protecting personal details
- Passwords and Passcodes
- Cyberbullies and trolls
- Private social media
- Cyber strangers
- I'm in trouble
- Cyber criminals
- Pop-ups and pitfalls
- Viruses and malware
- Digital quiz